Environmental Lifestyle Guide

For Grade 12 Students

VOL.9 OF 11

Professional

Jahangir Asadi

Vancouver, BC CANADA

Published by: Silosa Consulting Group Inc.
Vancouver, BC **CANADA**
Email: Info@Silosa.ca
www.silosa.ca

Ordering Information:
Quantity sales. Special discounts are available on quantity purchases by universities, schools, corporations, associations, and others. For details, contact the "Sales Department" at the above mentioned email address.

Environmental lifestyle Guide Vol.9 for Grade.12/J.Asadi —1st ed.
ISBN: 978-1-990451-83-6

Contents

We hope that, 10,000 years from now, future generations will be able to see flowers that provide bees with nectar and pollen and...
BEES provide flowers with the means to reproduce by spreading pollen from flower to flower,....

Jahangir Asadi

This book is dedicated to my professor, Dr.Bijan Esfandiari

Introduction

This book is part of an eleven volume series that is meant to be a standard textbook series, for grades 9 to 12. TTAIN & ESFK & SCG improves quality of life and reduces environmental degradation by fostering new consumption patterns and sustainable lifestyles through International Cooperative Extension Service programs at houses, offices, schools and libraries all over the globe.

Climate change is real. Therefore people have the potential to make a difference now and for future generations. This book provides climate science basics, including the roles that lifestyles and populations play in the climate scenario, the significance of carbon footprints, and an overview of the current climate situation. The manual has been categorized based on humanity's needs starting first with food and ending with tourism. The manual then illustrates the difference between adaptation (taking steps to live with the changes) and mitigation (taking steps to slow the rate of change.)

Adaptation examples include food, energy, transportation, recreation. Mitigation focuses on effectively engaging with local governments, through serving on advisory boards, communicating with public officials, educational institutes, schools, universities, libraries and leading communities towards climate change actions.

One useful way to mitigate climate change is through increasing public knowledge to better understand the impact of the rate of change on plants and animals. This is crucial for preserving species; and for assessing potential insects and disease outbreaks in agriculture, natural resources and public health.

Taking personal action is a key element of this manual.

Citizens are challenged to consume 20% fewer resources, to bring world consumption levels down as much as possible. Readers are given 12 practical steps to take to make the changes. The resources section provides additional information, and readers are encouraged to contact the author for further questions.

As an accessibility action, we have provided Online international courses on climate change control as well. You can access the courses via the following link:

http://TopTenAward.org

SILOSA Consulting Group (SCG)

Silosa Consulting Group (SCG) was established to provide outstanding consulting services of management system & educational standards to individuals, groups, companies, schools, and organizations all over the globe. SCG is publishing an "Environmental Lifestyle Guide " book series as a standard textbook related to increasing environmental awareness of students means being aware of the natural environment and making choices that benefit the earth, rather than hurt it. Vol.1 to 11 (for grades 9 to 12) providing some of the ways to practice environmental awareness include: **Recycling**, **Conserving energy and water**, **Reuse, Activism, and others**.

SCG book publishing services and distribution services are connected to over 39,000 booksellers worldwide, including Apple, Amazon, Barnes & Noble, Indigo, Google Play Books, and many more. SCG has enough experiences to help create new and effective environmental educational programmes in different countries all over the world. For more detail, visit our website : http://silosa.ca and/or send your enquirer to the following email:

info@silosa.ca

CHAPTER 1

About ISO 14000 for Students

The International Organization for Standardization is an independent, non-governmental organization, the members of which are the standards organizations of the 165 member countries. It is the world's largest developer of voluntary international standards and it facilitates world trade by providing common standards among nations. More than twenty thousand standards have been set, covering everything from manufactured products and technology to food safety, agriculture, and healthcare.

Kids ISO 14000s
"Kids ISO 14000s" is a new environmental education program for children, based on ISO 14000s, which is international standard for environmental management. Primary aims of this program are: -
1. To teach and train children how to manage the environmental issues (such as energy saving) by themselves through the working book and guide book of this program,
2. To certify those children who showed good accomplishment in the program from highly international authority (as is the case of ISO 14000s)
3. To network those children through the international network (Kids International Network), so that the children can work on the environment, internationally.

2. System of Kids ISO 14000s Program
The system of Kids ISO 14000s Program consists of
1. Operation Headquarter (ArTech).
2. Workbook, Guidebook (originally published by ArTech, and local versions are produced by each countries).
3. Eco-Kids-Instructors for local operation and evaluation of the performance of the children.
4. International accreditation committee for accreditation of accomplishment of the children, for certification of the Eco-Kids-Instructors, as well as overall checks of this program.
5. Linkage with international organizations (such as UNU, UNESCO, etc. …) And also national organizations

More information can be obtained :

www.ISO.org

Canada

Environmental Sustain for Future kids established in Vancouver, BC Canada in 2020. (ESFK) is an international ecolabel focused on taking care of environment for future of kids. ESFK defined as 'self-declared' environmental claims made by manufacturers and businesses based on ISO 14020 series of standards, the claimant can declare the environmental objectives and targets in relation to taking care of environment for future kids.
However, this declaration will be verifiable.

Environmental Sustain for Future Kids
Vancouver, BC CANADA

Email: info@esfk.org
Web: www.esfk.org

How can Professionals be 'Eco-friendly'

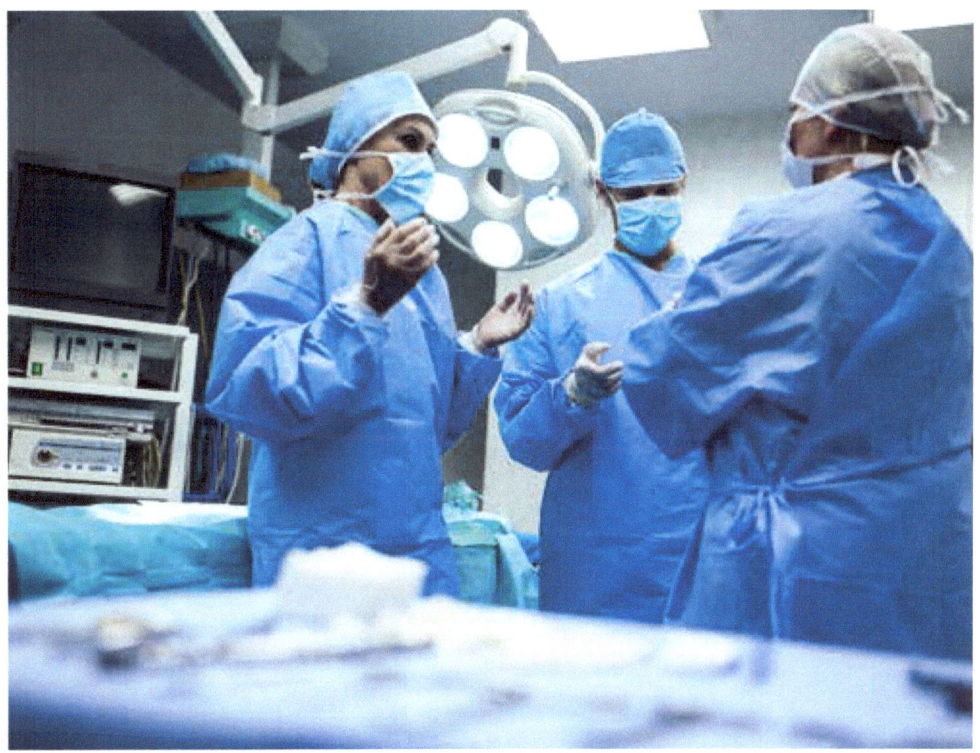

What is Being Environmentally Friendly? ... A good way would be to start with conserving water, driving less and walking more, consuming less energy, buying Ecolabelled and recycled products, eating locally grown vegetables, joining environmental groups to combat air pollution, creating less waste, planting more trees, and many more.

TEACHERS

How can teachers be eco friendly?

As a teacher, there are so many things you can do to make your classroom and school more green. From recycling, to planting gardens, to powering your school with solar panels to getting a green seal, the ideas are endless.

TTAIN has generated a list of 7 ways to go green in the classroom. This list covers everything from ideas for classroom décor to ways to make your classroom more energy efficient. Plus teaching students about green practices now creates a lifelong interest in saving the planet. These ideas help lay the groundwork for a green school and classroom. What will you start today?

1. Lead a green club

Find students who are interested in making their school more eco-friendly. Help them set a small goal to get started and then encourage them to think of more big picture ideas.

2. Prepare appropriate Text books

Textbooks are especially helpful for beginning Eco-friendly teachers. The material to be covered and the design of each lesson are carefully spelled out in detail. Eco-friendly Textbooks (such as Environmental Lifestyle Guide G.9-12) accompanied with a knowledge test, provide organized eco-friendly units of work. This series of textbooks gives you all the plans and lessons you need to cover to create a more green school environment. Order your package right now via (www.ecofriendlyeducation.com).

3.Create a Recycling Center

A classroom recycling center is a great way to get kids excited about recycling. You can reduce the burden of sorting materials by designating a student "recycle ranger" to make sure everything is in its place.

4.Apply for grants

Find and apply for grants that offer financial support for green-school initiatives. There are lots of opportunities.

5.Green Mantras

Unify your classroom theme by adopting a green mantra. Display it prominently in your classroom. Ideas include: My choices make a difference. We have the power to make a difference in the world.

6. Eco-Friendly School Supplies

Promote using Eco friendly school supplies that are better for the environment.

7. Energy Efficiency in the Classroom

Turn off heating or cooling units and open the windows when the weather is nice. Enjoy the fresh air!

PILOTS

How can pilots be eco friendly?

Focusing on pilots' pre-flight, in-flight and post-flight behaviours and throwing in a few small incentives, the study led to some huge fuel savings and an unexpected jump in work satisfaction for many of the pilots. While commercial aviation accounts for 2.5 percent of global carbon emissions, the industry is taking strides to reduce its carbon footprint.

Eco friendly Pilots usually:

- Using less power for takeoff
- Taxiing with just one engine
- Maximizing cruising altitudes and winds
- More efficient circling
- Using less fuel to descend
- **Recommendation to all friends and family to have " Climate Change Control Manual "Published by Top Ten Award International Network in their home and/or offices)**
- Look at Environmental Labels

LAWYERS

How can lawyers be eco friendly?

While the world is still not far from the brink of irreversible damage from climate change, more and more companies–both big and small–are taking the necessary steps to become more sustainable. The same is true for law firms. As sustainability movements encourage people and businesses to go green, law firms are also stepping up to the plate. Here are some of the best ways law firms can achieve sustainability in their

offices:

- Reduce unnecessary paper use
- Choose sustainable office supplies (Refer to Vol.6 stationery)
- Minimize single-use cups and bottles (Refer to International Environmental Labelling Vol.1 Chapter 7)
- Minimize travel
- Invest in energy efficiency (Refer to Environmental Lifestyle Guide Vol.2 of 11),
- **Recommendation to all friends and family to have " Climate Change Control Manual "Published by Top Ten Award International Network in their home and/or offices)**
- Look at Environmental Labels

Advertising Professionals

How can advertising professionals be eco friendly?

Eco-friendly advertising or marketing refers to selling products or services based on their environmental benefits. These offerings may be environmentally friendly in themselves, or their production process is somehow ecologically responsible. Eco-friendly advertising campaigns highlight these benefits and share them with your consumers. Here are a few tips that will help you create a successful, eco-friendly advertising and marketing strategy:

- Focus on the Benefits
- **Recommendation to all friends and family to have " Climate Change Control Manual "Published by Top Ten Award International Network in their home and/or offices)**
- Think Locally
- Support Environmental Initiatives
- Always Be Transparent
- Look at Environmental Labels

ARCHITECTS

How can architects be eco friendly?

By using trees, plants, and grasses that are native to the area, architects can greatly reduce irrigation needs. Landscaping can also be used as part of a passive energy strategy. By planting trees that shade the roof and windows during the hottest time of the day, solar heat gain inside the building can be reduced.

Here are some of the best ways architects can achieve sustainability in their projects:

- Design in airtightness - Eco frienedly Design of buildings
- Use enough insulation - most buildings are built with too little
- Use the buildings thermal mass to best effect
- Choose the building materials with Ecolabels
- Make the best use of natural light
- Deploy renewable technologies only after your shell design is complete
- **Recommendation to all friends and family to have " Climate Change Control Manual "Published by Top Ten Award International Network in their home and/or offices)**

ACCOUNTANTS

How can accountants be eco friendly?

When it comes to the sustainable development of your accounting and bookkeeping business, one of the biggest things you should start with is reducing the amount of paper you use. Consider scanning your important documents and converting them into digital documents instead.

Green Accounting and Bookkeeping: 7 Tips for Your Business:

- Go Paperless
- Opt to Hold Virtual Meetings More Often
- Watch Your Electricity, gas, water Consumption for a planning reducing
- Use Recycled or Recyclable Office Supplies
- **Recommendation to all friends and family to have " Climate Change Control Manual "Published by Top Ten Award International Network in their home and/or offices)**
- Be Conscious of Your Transportation Choices
- Look at Environmental Labels

ENGINEERS

How can engineers be eco friendly?

Green engineering is the design, commercialization, and use of processes and products in a way that reduces pollution, promotes sustainability, and minimizes risk to human health and the environment without sacrificing economic viability and efficiency.

There's often an emphasis on businesses being environmentally responsible in their operations, but everyday professionals have a role to play too.

Here are the top ways that engineering professionals can be environmentally friendly:

- Avoid Paper Waste
- Get Educated Online
- Suggest Solutions at Work
- Use The Right Tech
- Choose the engineering materials with Ecolabels
- **Recommendation to all friends and family to have " Climate Change Control Manual "Published by Top Ten Award International Network in their home and/or offices)**
- Conserve Energy

CONSULTANTS

How can consultants be eco friendly?

An environmental consultant's goal is to help others make informed decisions about policies or projects that will impact the environment.

In short, they gather information, analyze it, and provide their recommendations.

These consultants might provide plans for reducing waste or conserving energy. An eco consultant might even produce a viable roadmap towards switching over to renewable energy. An eco consultant might look for more ethical sources of materials and offer guidance on sustainable purchasing practices.

Eco consultants may provide a wide range of services to help companies become more sustainable. According to Eco-officiency, these services mostly involve environmental assessments and plans for corrective measures.

An eco consultant might, for example, assess how a company utilizes natural resources like energy, water, and carbon, while also investigating how they dispose of waste products or hazardous materials.

Human Resources Specialist

How can HR specialist be eco friendly?

Environmental sustainability will only be achieved if we all do our part. And that includes those of us who work in the HR industry. Here are the top ways that HR professionals can be environmentally friendly:

- Cut out paper waste
- Invest in reusables to eliminate single-use plastics
- Initiate employee volunteer opportunities to create a positive difference
- Get creative with end of week waste
- Try to recommend people who think eco friendly for hiring
- **Recommendation to all friends and family to have " Climate Change Control Manual "Published by Top Ten Award International Network in their home and/or offices)**
- Conserve Energy
- Be Conscious of employee Transportation Choices
- Look at Environmental Labels

RESEARCH & DEVELOPMENT

How can R & D specialist be eco friendly?

R&D has an important role in improving the environmental performance of industry – an important element in sustainable development. International Energy Agency figures indicate that technologies and best practices could save between 17 and 27% of current primary energy use in global industry. Putting International R&D at the service of sustainable development is essential to our future.

Innovative production has a vital role in the quest for sustainable development. The ambition of eco-efficiency is to close the loops in the life cycle, so business models must adapt. And we must teach people how to work with people in other fields. Sustainable development is both a challenge and an opportunity for the process industries in the world.

Key aspects include:

- Implementing research for sustainable development
- Designing research policy for sustainable development
- Measuring the contribution of research to sustainable development

PSYCHOLOGIST

How can psychologist be eco friendly?

Conducting research on messages that motivate people to change their behavior. Spreading the word about environmental solutions. Uncovering why people may not adopt positive behaviors. Encouraging people to rethink their positions in the natural world.

Social psychology's contribution to a sustainable, flourishing future will come partly through its consciousness-transforming insights into adaptation and comparison. Conservation psychology is not only concerned with the ways psychology can contribute to protecting the natural environment, but also with how attention to the natural environment can contribute to psychology. ... It is well known, for example, that environmental toxins can have direct impacts on human health.

Here are the top ways that psychologists can act environmentally friendly:

- Effects on human behavior
- Infloencing on the public opinion about climate change, and
- Ways to modify the human sources of climate change

PHARMACIST

How can pharmacist be eco friendly?

Pharmacists can help to ensure that unused medications are returned to the pharmacy and disposed of appropriately, through hazardous waste companies. 3,4 By educating patients on proper disposal, pharmacists contribute significantly to preventing medications from entering the water supply.

Both recycling and waste reduction are important to making pharmacy practice more sustainable. Though patient education, recycling, and paperless communication methods are feasible short-term options, there are still a few barriers towards implementing these sustainable practices.

Here are the top ways that pharmacist can be environmentally friendly:

- Avoid Paper Waste
- Conserve energy (Refer to International Environmental Labelling Book series Vol.2 Energy)
- Encourage green logistics
- Sell eco-friendly products (Refer to International Environmental Labelling Book series Vol.4 and Vol.5)
- Order larger bottles
- Reuse pill containers
- Recycle (Refer to International Environmental Labelling Book series Vol.1 Chapter 7)
- **Recommendation to all friends and family to have " Climate Change Control Manual "Published by Top Ten Award International Network book in their home and/or offices)**

COMMERCIAL BANKERS

How can commercial banker be eco friendly?

By allowing card holders to use digital technologies to manage their finances, banks and other payment providers are providing a sustainable alternative to paper statements and physical bank branches. ... with innovative, more seamless experience, but it also allows banks to reduce their carbon footprint.

Here are the top ways that commercial bankers can act environmentally friendly:

- Moving away from paper
- Using sustainable materials and partnering with green suppliers
- Providing customer insight about their carbon footprint
- **Recommendation to all friends and family to have " Climate Change Control Manual "Published by Top Ten Award International Network book in their home and/or offices)**
- Conserve Energy
- Encourage green logistics
- Choosing eco-friendly products

DOCTORS & NURSES

How can doctors and nurses be eco friendly?

Over the past seven years, hospitals are becoming more eco-friendly, seeking to lighten their environmental footprints. The benefits are tremendous! Among them are safer patients, less wastefulness, and lower facility operating costs.

Here are the top ways that doctors & nurses can be environmentally friendly:

- Avoid Paper Waste
- Conserve energy (Refer to International Environmental Labelling Book series Vol.2 Energy)
- Encourage green logistics
- Choosing eco-friendly products (Refer to International Environmental Labelling Book series Vol.4 and Vol.5)
- Order larger bottles
- Reuse pill containers
- Recycle (Refer to Environmental Lifestyle Guide Book series Vol.1.
- **Recommendation to all friends and family to have " Climate Change Control Manual "Published by Top Ten Award International Network book in their home and/or offices)**
- Reducing, treating, and safely disposing of waste

We recommend to all friends and family to have Recommendation to all friends and family to have " Climate Change Control Manual " Published by Top Ten Award International Network in their home and/or offices)

KNOWLEDGE TESTS

1) Eco-Friendly School Supplies. Promote using Eco friendly school supplies that are better for the environment.
A) True
B) False
ANSWER:

2) The top ways that psychologists can act environmentally friendly:
A) Effects on human behavior
B) Infloencing on the public opinion about climate change
C) Ways to modify the human sources of climate change
D) All of them
ANSWER:

3) Your school with solar panels to getting a green seal, the ideas are endless.
A) True
B) False
ANSWER:

4) How can lawyers be eco friendly? While the world is still not far from the brink of irreversible damage from climate change, more and more companies–both big and small–are taking the necessary steps to become more sustainable.
A) True
B) False
ANSWER:

5) A classroom recycling center is a great way to get kids excited about recycling.
A) True
B) False
ANSWER:

6) Top ways that pharmacist can be environmentally friendly:
A) Avoid Paper Waste
B) Conserve Energy
C) Encourage green logistics
D) Order larger bottles
E) Reuse pill containers
F) All of them
ANSWER:

7) An environmental consultant's goal is to help others make informed decisions about policies or projects that will impact the environment.
A) True
B) False
ANSWER:

8) As a teacher, there are so many things you can do to make your classroom and school more green. From recycling, to planting gardens, to powering your school with solar panels to getting a green seal, the ideas are endless.
A) True
B) False
ANSWER:

9) A classroom recycling center is a great way to get kids excited about recycling. You can reduce the burden of sorting materials by designating a student "recycle ranger" to make sure everything is in its place.
A) True
B) False
ANSWER:

10) Focusing on pilots' pre-flight, in-flight and post-flight behaviours and throwing in a few small incentives, the study led to some huge fuel savings and an unexpected jump in work satisfaction for many of the pilots
A) True
B) False
ANSWER:

11) Eco friendly Pilots usually:
A) Using less power for takeoff
B) Taxiing with just one engine
C) Maximizing cruising altitudes and winds
D) All of them
ANSWER:

12) As sustainability movements encourage people and businesses to go green, law firms are also stepping up to the plate.
A) True
B) False
ANSWER:

13) By planting trees that shade the roof and windows during the hottest time of the day, solar heat gain inside the building can be reduced
A) True
B) False
ANSWER:

14) Putting International R&D at the service of sustainable development is essential to our future.
A) True
B) False
ANSWER:

15) Here are the top ways that engineering professionals can be environmentally friendly:
A) Avoid Paper Waste
B) Get Educated Online
C) Suggest Solutions at Work
D) Choose the engineering materials with Ecolabels
E) Conserve Energy
F) All of them
ANSWER:

16) Over the past seven years, hospitals are becoming more eco-friendly, seeking to lighten their environmental footprints. The benefits are tremendous! Among them are safer patients, less wastefulness, and lower facility operating costs.
A) True
B) False
ANSWER:

17) Both recycling and waste reduction are important to making pharmacy practice more sustainable. Though patient education, recycling, and paperless communication methods are feasible short-term options, there are still a few barriers towards implementing these sustainable practices.
A) True
B) False
ANSWER:

18) Eco consultants may provide a wide range of services to help companies become more sustainable. According to Eco-officiency, these services mostly involve environmental assessments and plans for corrective measures.
A) True
B) False
ANSWER:

19) An eco consultant might, for example, assess how a company utilizes natural resources like energy, water, and carbon, while also investigating how they dispose of waste products or hazardous materials.
A) True
B) False
ANSWER:

20) Environmental sustainability will only be achieved if we all do our part.
A) True
B) False
ANSWER:

Bibliography:

Asadi, J., "International Environmental Labelling, Economic Consequencies, Export Magazine, July 2001

Asadi, J. 2008. Mobile Phone as management systems tools, ISO Magazine, Vol.8, No.1

Asadi, J., Eco-Labelling Standards, National Standard Magazine, Sep. 2004.

Barbieux, D.; Padula, A.D. Paths and Challenges of New Technologies: The Case of Nanotechnology-Based Cosmetics Development in Brazil. Adm. Sci. 2018, 8, 16.

CHOI, J.P. Brand Extension as Informational Leverage. Review of Eco- nomic Studies, Vol. 65 (1998), pp. 655-669.

Corrado, M., (1989), The Greening Consumer in Britain, MORI, London

Corrado, M., (1997), Green Behaviour – Sustainable Trends, Sustainable Lives?, MORI, london, accessed via countries. Manila, Asian Development Bank 33p.

Cosmetics, Perfume, & Hygiene in Ancient Egypt. Available online: https://www.ancient.eu/article/1061/cosmetics-perfume--hygiene-in-ancient-egypt/

He Z, Xu J X 1993 Evalustion and measurement of Landscape greening benefit J.Chinese Landscape Architecture. 03 46-51

Davies, Clive. Chief, Design for the Environment Program, EPA March 24, 2009.

EIP-AGRI network at www.eip-agri.eu

The Family Butterfly Book by Rick Mikula. Storey Publishing,

Federal Trade Commission, "Sorting Out Green Advertising Claims." http://www.ftc.gov/bcp/edu/pubs/consumer/general/gen02.shtm (March 26, 2009, March 27, 2009)

MSNBC, "Do You Know What's in Your Cleaning Products?" http://today.msnbc.msn.com/id/29663739/ (March 17, 2009)

Ooyen, Carla. Research Manager with Nutrition Business Journal. Personal correspondence. March 19, 2009.

Tekin, Jenn. Marketing Manager with Packaged Facts & SBI. Personal correspondence. March 17, 2009.

University of California - Berkeley. http://berkeley.edu/news/media/releases/2006/05/22_householdchemicals.shtml (March 26, 2009)

Feenstra, R.C. "Exact Hedonic Price Indexes," Review of Economics and Statistics 77 (1995): 634-653.

Feenstra, R.C., and J.A. Levinsohn. "Estimating Markups and Market Conduct with Multidimensional Product Attributes," Review of Economic Studies (62 (1995): 19-52.

Forest Stewardship Council: "Principles and criteria for forest stewardship" Document 1.2: <http://www.fscoax.org>

Forsyth, K. 1999. Will consumers pay more for certified wood products? Journal of Forestry 97 (2) : 18-22.

Freeman, A. M III. The Measurement of Environmental and Resource Values. Theory and Methods. Washington D.C.: Resource for the Future, 1993.

Friends of the Earth, 1993. Timber certification and eco-labeling. London, FOE:

Geetha Margret Soundri, "Ecofriendly Antimicrobial Finishing of Textiles Using Natural

Halvorsen, R. and R. Palmquist. "The Interpretation of Dummy Variables in Semilogarithmic Equations." American Economic Review 70:474-75 (1980).

Imhoff, Dan, and Grose, Lynda, and Carra, Roberto., "Organic Cotton Exhibit," Mimeo. Simple Life and distributed the Texas Organic Cotton Marketing Cooperative, O'Donnell, Texas (1996).

Imhoff, Dan. "Growing Pains: Organic Cotton Tests the Fibre of Growers and Manufacturers Alike," reprinted on Simple Life's web page (simplelife.com), but first printed by Farmer to Farmer, December 1995.

IISO 14020, ISO 14021,ISO 14024,ISO 14025, International Organization for Standardization.

Kennedy, P.E. "Estimation with Correctly Interpreted Dummy Variables in Semilogarithmic Equations," American Economic Review 71: 801 (1981).

Kirchho®, S., (2000), Green Business and Blue Angels.

Labeling Issues, Policies and Practices Worldwide.

Lamport, L. 1998. The cast of (timber) certifiers: who are they? International J. Ecoforestry 11(4): 118-122.

Large Scale impoverishment of Amazonian forests by logging and fire. 1999.

Lathrop, K.W. and Centner, T.J. 1998. Eco-labeling and ISO 14000: An analysis of US regulatory systems and issues concerning adoption of type II standards. Environmental

Lee, J. et al. 1996. Trade related environmental measures; sizing and comparing impacts.

Lehtonen, Markku. 1997. Criteria in Environmental Labeling: A comparative Analysis on Environmental Criteria in Selected Labeling Schemes. Geneva, UNEP. 148p.

LIEBI, T. Trusting Labels: A Matter of Numbers? Working Paper Uni versity of Bern, No. 0201 (2002).

Lindstrom, T. 1999. Forest Certification: The View from Europe's NIPFs. Journal of Forestry 97(3): 25-31. London

Losey, J.E., Rayor, L.S. & Carter, M.E. 1999. Transgenic pollen harms monarch larvae. Nature 399 20 May): p.214.

Management 22 (2) : 163-172.

Mattoo, A. and H. V. Singh, (1994), Eco-Labelling: Policy Considera-Michaels, R. G., and V. K. Smith. "Market Segmentation And Valuing Amenities With Hedonic Models: The Case Of Hazardous Waste Sites," Journal of Urban Economics, 1990 28(2), 223-242.

Nicholson-Lord, D., (1993) 'Tis the Season to be Green, The Independent, 20 December

Nuttall, N., (1993), Shoppers can cross green products off their lists, The Times, 3 July OCDE/GD(97)105. Paris, OECD. 81p.

OECD. "Ec-labelling: Actual Effects of Selected Programmes," OCDE/GD (97) 105, 1997, Paris. (available on line at http://www.oecd.org/env/eco/books.htm#trademono)

OECD. 1997a. Case study on eco-labeling schemes. Paris, OECD (30 Dec):

OECD. 1997b. Eco-labeling: Actual Effects of Selected Programs.

Osborne, L. "Market Structure, Hedonic Models, and the Valuation of Environmental Amenities." Unpublished Ph.D. dissertation. North Carolina State University, 1995.

Osborne, L., and V. K. Smith. "Environmental Amenities, Product Differentiation, and market Power," Mimeo, 1997.

Palmquist, R. B., F. M. Roka, and T.Vukina. "Hog Operations, Environmental Effects, and Residential Property Values," Land Economics 73(1), (1997): 114-24.

Palmquist, R.B. "Hedonic Methods," in J.B Braden and C.D. Kolstad, eds. Measuring the Demand for Environmental Improvement. Amsterdam, NL: Elsevier, 1991.

Pento, T. 1997. Implementation of Public Green Procurement Programs (22-31) in Greener Purchasing: Opportunities and Innovations. Sheffield, Greenleaf Publ. 325 p.

Polak, J. and Bergholm, K. 1997. Eco-labeling and trade: a cooperative approach (Jan.): Policy in a Green Market. Environmental and Resource Economics 22, 419-

Poore, M.E.D. et al. 1989. No timber without trees. London, Earthscan. 352p.

Raff, D. M.G., and M. Trajtenberg. "Quality-Adjusted Prices for the American Automobile Industry: 1906-1940." NBER Working Paper Series, Working Paper No. 5035, February 1995.

Roberts, J. T. 1998. Emerging global environment standards: prospects and perils. Journal of Developing Societies 14 (1): 144-163.

Ross, B. 1997. Eco-friendly procurement training course for UN HCR. : 126 p.

Salzman, J. 1997. Informing the Green Consumer: The Debate over the Use and Abuse of Environmental Labels. Journal of Industrial Ecology 1 (2): 11-22.

Sanders, W. 1997. Environmentally Preferable Purchasing: The US Experience (946-960) in Greener Purchasing: Opportunities and Innovations. Sheffield, Greenleaf Publ. 325p.

Sayre, D. 1996. Inside ISO 14000: The competitive advantage of environmental management. Delray Beach FL., St. Lucie Press. 232p.

SHAPIRO, C. Premiums for High Quality Products as Returns to Reputa- tion. Quarterly Journal of Economics, Vol. 98, No. 4 (1983), pp. 659-680.

Stillwell, M. and van Dyke, B. 1999. An activists handbook on genetically modified organisms and the WTO. Washington DC., The Consumer's Choice Council: 20 p.

Semenzato, A.; Costantini, A.; Meloni, M.; Maramaldi, G.; Meneghin, M.; Baratto, G. Formulating O/W Emulsions with Plant-Based Actives: A Stability Challenge for an Eective Product. Cosmetics 2018, 5, 59.

Teisl, M. F., B. Roe, and R. L. Hicks. "Can Eco-labels tune a market? Evidence from dolphin-safe labeling," Presented paper at the 1997 American Agricultural Economics Association Meetings, Toronto.

www.futureplc.com

He F C, Li Y, Yang X M, Qin F 2017 Exploration on the development path of old industrial base transition:taking Xuzhou city as an example to establish a national Eco-garden city J. Chinese Landscape Architecture. 33 91-95

Tibor, T. and Feldman, I. 1995. ISO 14000: a guide to the new environmental management standards. Burr Ridge Ill., Irwin Professional Publ. 250 p.

Du L P 2009 Some thoughts on the present situation of the application of ground cover plants J. Northern Horticulture. 08 229-231

Du H Z, Song W 1996 A brief analysis of ecological benefits of greening in Song Qingling cemetery J. Journal of Jiangsu Forestry & Technology. S1 88-91

Townsend, M. 1998. Making things greener: motivations and influences in the greening of manufacturing. Aldershot, England, Ashgate Publisher. 203p.

U.S. Energy Information Administration, What is U.S. Electricity Generation by Energy Source?, Retrieved From: https://www.eia.gov/tools/faqs/faq.php?id=427&t=3

U.S. Energy Information Administration, Biomass Explained, Retrieved From: https://www.eia.gov/energyexplained/?page=biomass_home

U.S. Environmental Protection Agency. National Water Quality Fact Inventory: 1990 Report to Congress. EPA 503-9-92-006, Apr. 1992.

UK Eco-labelling Board website, accessed via http://www.ecosite.co.uk/Ecolabel-UK/

US EPA, 1993. The use of life-cycle assessment in environmental labeling. Washington, D.C., US Environmental Protection Agency (742-R-93-003 September).

Wang L Y 1994 How to improve the ecological benefits in the construction of Jinan garden J. Chinese Landscape Architecture. 03 56-58+55

US EPA, 1998. Environmental labeling: issues, policies, and practices worldwide.

US EPA, 1999. Comprehensive procurement guidelines (CPG) program. Washington, D.C., US Environmental Protection Agency: <www.epa.gov/cpg>

US EPA, 1999. Environmentally preferable purchasing program: Private sector pioneers: How companies are incorporating environmentally preferable purchases. Washington, D.C.,

USG, 1993. Federal acquisition, recycling, and waste prevention. Washington DC., Executive Order: (20 October).

USG, 1998. Greening the government through waste prevention, recycling, and federal acquisition. Washington, D.C., Executive Order 13101 (September).

Kijjoa, A.; Sawangwong, P. Drugs and Cosmetics from the Sea. Mar. Drugs 2004, 2, 73–82. [CrossRef]

Wang, J.; Pan, L.; Wu, S.; Lu, L.; Xu, Y.; Zhu, Y.; Guo, M.; Zhuang, S. Recent Advances on Endocrine Disrupting Eects of UV Filters. Int. J. Environ. Res. Public Health 2016, 13, 782.

Bilal, A.I.; Tilahun, Z.; Shimels, T.; Gelan, Y.B.; Osman, E.D. Cosmetics Utilization Practice in Jigjiga Town, Eastern Ethiopia: A Community Based Cross-Sectional Study. Cosmetics 2016, 3, 40.

Ting, C.T.; Hsieh, C.M.; Chang, H.-P.; Chen, H.-S. Environmental Consciousness and Green Customer Behavior: The Moderating Roles of Incentive Mechanisms. Sustainability 2019, 11, 819.

Chen, K.; Deng, T. Research on the Green Purchase Intentions from the Perspective of Product Knowledge. Sustainability 2016, 8, 943.

Wang, H.; Ma, B.; Bai, R. How Does Green Product Knowledge Eectively Promote Green Purchase Intention? Sustainability 2019, 11, 1193.

Nguyen, T.T.H.; Yang, Z.; Nguyen, N.; Johnson, L.W.; Cao, T.K. Greenwash and Green Purchase Intention: The Mediating Role of Green Skepticism. Sustainability 2019, 11, 2653.

Cinelli, P.; Coltelli, M.B.; Signori, F.; Morganti, P.; Lazzeri, A. Cosmetic Packaging to Save the Environment: Future Perspectives. Cosmetics 2019, 6, 26.

Eixarch, H.; Wyness, L.; Siband, M. The Regulation of Personalized Cosmetics in the EU. Cosmetics 2019, 6, 29.

CANADA SILVER BEAVER BADGE

Participate in our Online Classes to earn these exclusive digital badges!
www.toptenaward.org

Design & Development by:

Tara Asadi

CANADA BRONZE BEAVER BADGE

Participate in our Online Classes to earn these exclusive digital badges!
www.toptenaward.org

Design & Development by:

Tara Asadi

CANADA GOLD BEAVER BADGE

Participate in our Online Classes to earn these exclusive digital badges!

Design & Development by:

Tara Asadi

Environmental Lifestyle Guide

For Grade 9

For Grade 10

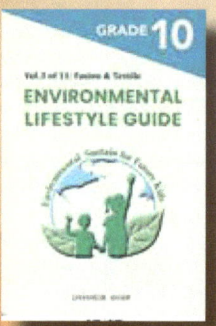
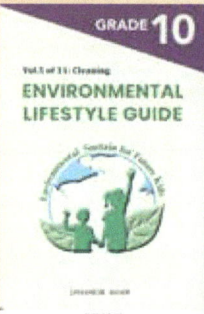
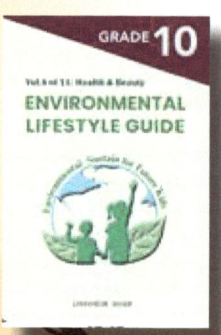

Plus Online Certification Tests via:
https://toptenaward.org

Standard Text Books

For Grade 11

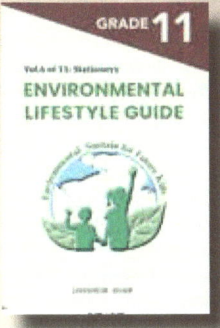  

For Grade 12

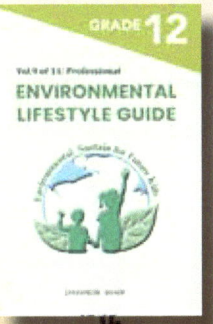 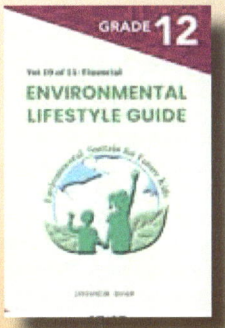 

**Environmental Lifestyle Guide
Standard Text Book**
For Students Grade 9 to 12
Available in more than
39,000 Bookstores
all over the globe.
https://ecofriendlyeducation.com

**Cooperation by:
Top Ten Award International Network
&
Environmental Sustain for Future Kids**